Follow That Star

9 Christmas songs in close harmony
S.A.T.B.

Edited and arranged by: Peter Gritton

Have Yourself A Merry Little Christmas 3
Hugh Martin and Ralph Blane

Winter Wonderland 6
Dick Smith and Felix Bernard

Follow That Star 18
Peter Gritton

An Olde Rhyme 23
Peter Gritton

Santa Claus Is Coming To Town 29
Haven Gillespie and J. Fred Coot

Mary's Boy Child 40
Jester Hairston

Just Another Star 50
Karl Jenkins and Carol Barratt

The Christmas Song 56
Mel Tormé and Robert Wells

Deck The Hall 60
Peter Gritton

Exclusive distributors:
Music Sales Limited,
Newmarket Road, Bury St. Edmunds, Suffolk, IP33 3YB.

This book © Copyright 1989 by
Chester Music Limited
UK ISBN 0.7119.1967.4.
Order No. CH 55953.

Printed in the United Kingdom by
Caligraving Limited.

CHESTER MUSIC
A division of Music Sales Limited,

CHORAL CONNECTION

Foreword

This collection of popular Christmas tunes is designed to be enjoyable to sing whilst
providing a challenge. The wide range of songs can be performed either in the order in which they are set,
or as a smaller set in the order of your choice, with no danger of monotony.
There is a great variety of texture and the melody-line has been shared amongst the voices as fairly as possible,
with perhaps a slight tendency towards the sopranos and baritones!

Arranger's Notes

1. Breathing. Wherever possible, stagger the breathing in longer phrases, unless
the text and the music naturally allow for a breath. This will preserve the fluency, especially in the "instrumental"
background sounds like *ooh* and *mm*. The sign ‿ below the text implies that no breath should be taken;
sometimes this may contradict the punctuation (e.g. end of "Mary's Boy Child", page 49).
, above the stave indicates a breathing mark for all voices
(e.g. throughout "Have Yourself A Merry Little Christmas", page 3).

2. Dynamics have, on the whole, have been layered in order to help bring out
important melodic lines. Further dynamics may be added to give these lines more of a chance over an
often rather rich close-harmony sound. As a rule, never over-sing –
hence the occasional direction: "*f* dolce"!

3. Ranges of individual parts usually allow for the possibility of having a few
Tenors, for instance, on the Baritone part, or a few Altos on the 2nd Soprano part, or *vice versa*.
This can be useful if you encounter problems with balance or with the numbers of singers available.

4. Please observe the subtleties of the "instrumental" sounds: e.g. there *is* a difference
between *dum* and *dmm! Ooh (doo)* and *ah (da)* imply a re-articulation within the appropriate vowel sound with
the suggested consonant (e.g. in the middle section of "Just Another Star", page 53),
just like re-bowing on a stringed instrument. The instrumental effects usually need no explanation,
but often an illusion to a particular instrument is helpful (*dmm* in the Bass part of
"Follow That Star", page 18, is like a plucked Double-Bass, and *ba-ba-ba-ba* . . . in bar 72 of
"Mary's Boy Child", page 48, is like fanfare brass).

5. "Christmas" is best pronounced without a "t".

Peter Gritton
July 1989

Have Yourself A Merry Little Christmas

Words and Music by Hugh Martin and Ralph Blane
Arranged by Peter Gritton

Winter Wonderland

Words by Dick Smith. Music by Felix Bernard
Arranged by Peter Gritton

A sleigh-bell or some such instrument may be used from bars 13–36 and 63–68, with a gentle shake on each crotchet.
In bar 80 a shake of about a minim may be made.

*Conglomerative effect should be ♪ ♩ ♪ ♩
                                         ding ding ding ding
'Ding' should be sung with a clear, wettish 'd', closing straight on to the 'ng' after a short vowel: almost 'tng'

*Swung: ♩. ♪ becomes ♩ ♪♪ (triplet)

13

16

Follow That Star

Words and Music by Peter Gritton

*All quaver and ♩. ♪ rhythms in this piece should be 'swung', with triplet feel. Thus the opening Tenor phrase should sound:

CH 55953

One dark and storm-y eve-ning, Through the wind and

rain, There came a sight worth see-ing, 'cause it

was-n't gon-na hap-pen a-gain: Three Kings

ba da 'n' doo da da

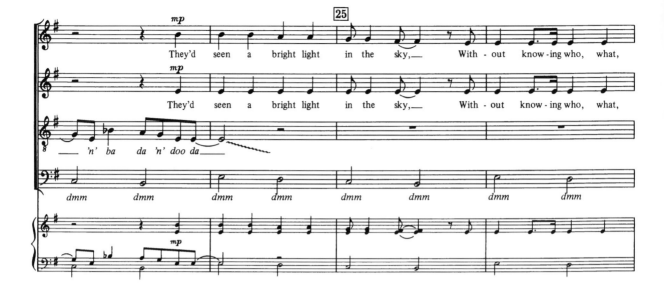

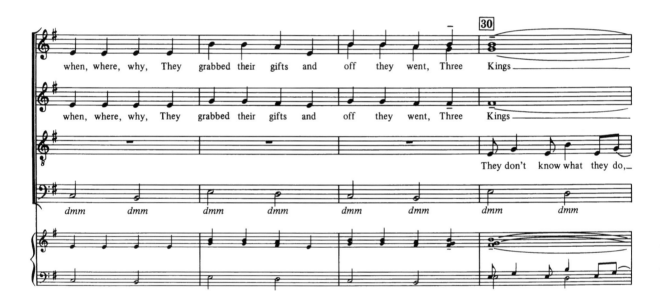

An Olde Rhyme

Words traditional and P. G. Music by Peter Gritton

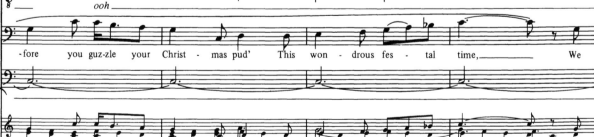

CH 55953

*This may be spoken by any member of the choir - in a manner of great character.

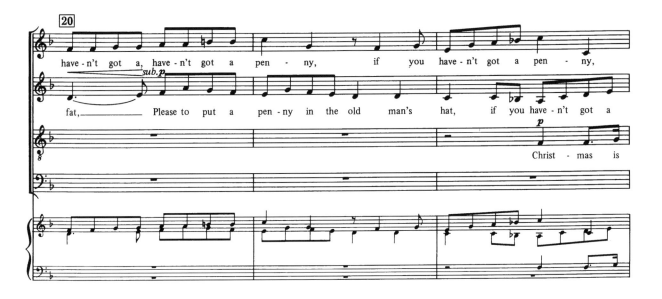

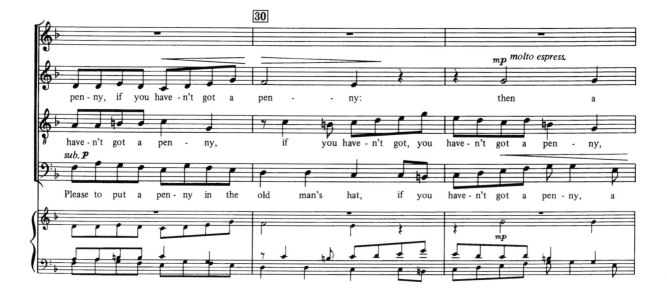

*ha'p'ny (half - penny), pronounced 'hayp - ny'

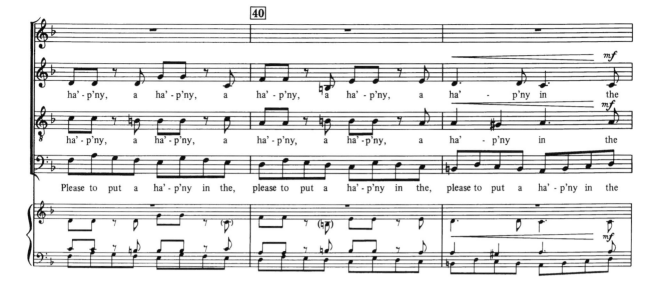

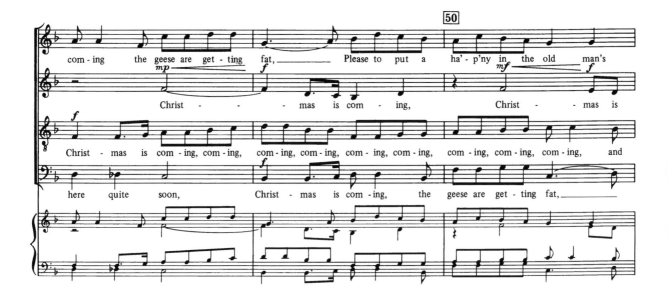

Santa Claus
Is Coming To Town

Words by Haven Gillespie. Music by Fred Coot
Arranged by Peter Gritton

I stopped off at the North Pole __ To spend a ho - li - day. __ I

(legato)
bop bop bop bop bop bop bop bop bop bop bop bop ba ba ba

(legato)
bop bop bop bop bop bop bop bop bop bop bop bop ba ba ba

(legato)
dum dum dum dum bop bop bop bop ba ba ba

mp
dum dum dum dum - ba

S called on dear old San - ta Claus To see what I could see. __ He

bop bop bop bop bop bop bop bop bop bop bop bop bop bop doo

A bop bop bop bop bop bop bop bop bop bop bop bop bop bop doo

T dum dum dum dum dum dum dum doo

(quasi percussion)
B dum dum dum dum dum dum dum ts

dum dum dum dum dum dum dum doo

From here to the end, all quaver and ♪♪ rhythms should be 'swung', with triplet feel.

Gon - na find out who's naught-y and nice, San - ta Claus is com - ing to

doo doo doo doo doo doo San - ta Claus is com - ing to

doo doo doo doo doo doo San - ta Claus is com - ing to

doo - by-doo doo-by-doo com - ing to

Gon - na find out who's naught-y and nice, San - ta Claus is com - ing to

bom bom bom bom San - ta's com - ing

town. la la la la

town. doo - by doo - by doo - by doo

town. la la la la

town. doo - by doo - by doo - by doo - by doo He sees you when you're

doo - by doo - by doo - by doo - by doo - by doo - by doo la la la la

dum dum dum dum dum ba ba

33

Mary's Boy Child

Words and Music by Jester Hairston
Arranged by Peter Gritton

*This song may be performed up a semitone if desired.

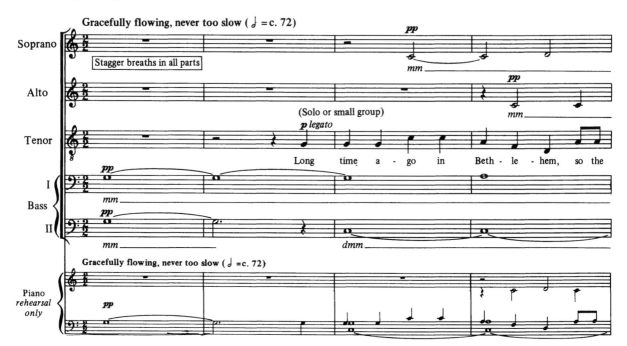

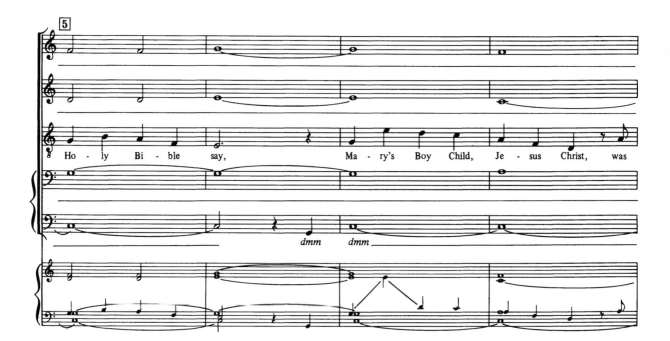

da da da Trum - pets sound and an - gels sing,

da da Trum - pets sound and an - gels sing,

(Solo) -cause of Christ - mas Day. Trum - pets sound, an - gels sing,

da da da da Trum - pets sound, an - gels sing,

Trum - pets sound, an - gels sing,

doo Trum - pets sound and the an - gels they sing, and

S Lis - ten to what they say, _____ ooh _____ doo doo doo doo doo

A Lis - ten to what they say, doo doo doo doo doo doo doo doo

T Lis - ten t'what they say, That Man will live for ev - er - more, be -

B Lis - ten t'what they say, ooh _____

Lis - ten t'what they say, _____ doo _____ doo _____

doo doo doo doo doo doo doo doo doo

find no place to born she child, not a sin - gle room was in sight.

doo doo doo doo doo doo doo doo doo doo

doo doo doo doo doo doo doo doo doo

doo doo doo doo doo doo doo doo doo

doo doo doo doo doo doo doo doo doo doo

45 (col tutti)

S

pp *sostenuto*

A Hark now hear the an - gels sing, a new King born to - day, And

pp *sostenuto*

T Hark now hear the an - gels sing, a new King born to - day, And

pp *sostenuto*

B Hark now hear the an - gels sing, a new King born to - day, And

pp *sostenuto*

Hark now hear the an - gels sing, a new King born to - day,

pp

in a man - ger cold and dark Ma - ry's lit - tle Boy was born.

doo doo doo doo doo doo doo doo doo doo doo doo doo doo doo

(Solo)
in a man - ger cold and dark Ma - ry's lit - tle Boy was born.

doo doo doo doo doo doo doo doo doo doo doo doo doo doo doo

doo doo doo doo doo doo doo doo doo doo doo doo doo doo doo

doo doo doo doo doo doo doo doo doo doo doo doo

mm

mm

(Solo)
Long time a - go in Beth - le - hem, so the

doo doo doo

doo doo doo doo doo doo mm

doo doo doo dmm dmm

Just Another Star

Words and Music by Karl Jenkins and Carol Barratt
Arranged by Peter Gritton

CH 55953

doo   doo   doo   doo   *mf dolce e sostenuto*   ah (dah)*

Found a ti - ny sta - ble just be - fore a child was born,   *mf dolce e sostenuto* ah (dah)
Up a - bove the sta - ble where the Ho - ly Child was born,

doo   doo   doo   doo   doo   *mf dolce e sostenuto* ah (dah)

Found a ti - ny sta - ble just be - fore a child was born,   *mf dolce e sostenuto* ah (dah)
Up a - bove the sta - ble where the Ho - ly Child was born,

doo   doo   doo doo   *mf dolce e sostenuto* ah (dah)

doo   doo   *mf ritmico* da da da da

mf

da da da da da da da   da da   da da da   da   da da   da

*The basic vowel is 'ah', articulated with a 'd' unless under a slur - this works like bowing on a stringed instrument.

The Christmas Song

Words and Music by Mel Tormé and Robert Wells
Arranged by Peter Gritton

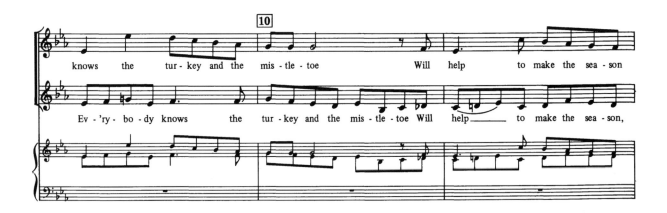

CH 55953

sleigh, And ev-'ry mo-ther's child _____ is gon-na spy _____ To see if

sleigh, _____ And ev-'ry mo - ther's child _____ is gon-na spy To

way, And ev - 'ry mo - ther's child will spy _____ To

way, And ev - 'ry child will spy _____ To

way, And ev - 'ry child will spy To

[25]

rein-deer real-ly know how to fly; And so we're of - fer - ing this sim-ple phrase To

see if they fly; _____ So we're of-fer-ing this phrase To

see if rein - deer fly; _____ we're of-fer ing this sim - ple phrase To

see, to see if _____ they fly; Here's a sim - ple phrase To

see if _____ they fly; So here's a sim - ple phrase To

Deck The Hall

Words traditional
Music by Peter Gritton

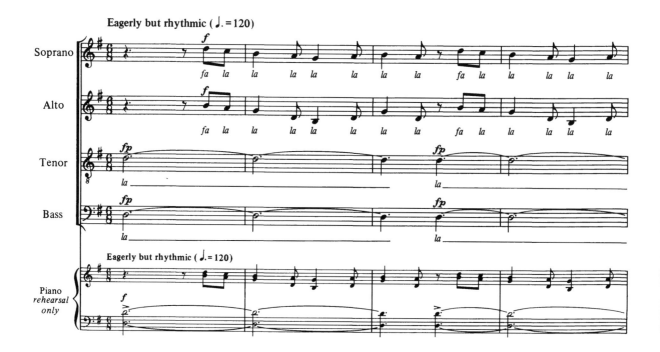

CH 55953

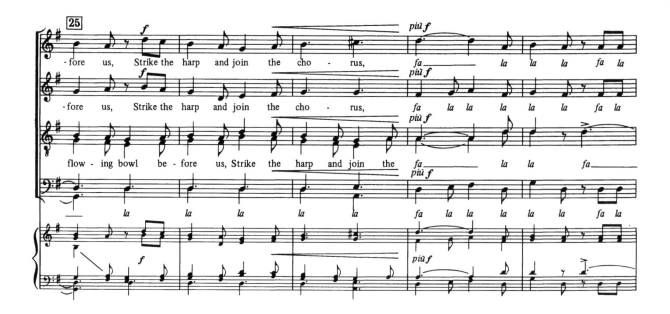

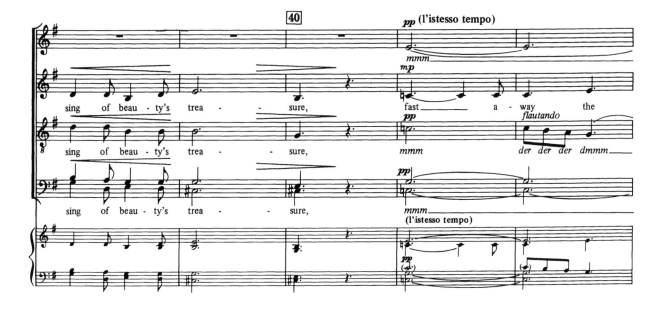

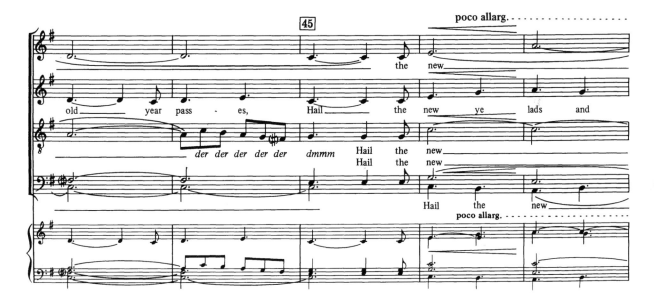

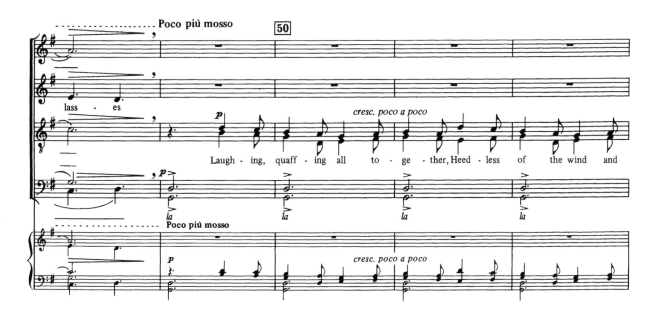

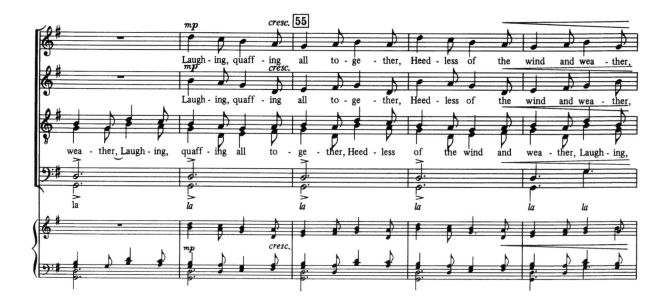

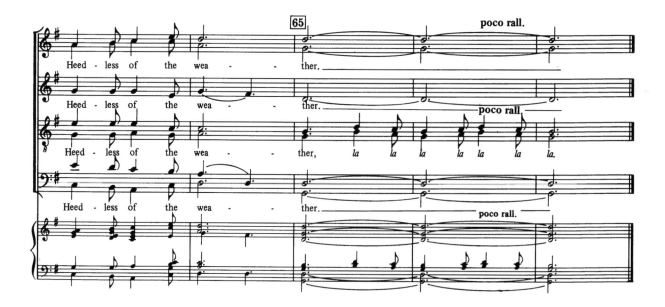